GOSPEL

Sierra Wilson

MY FAVORITE MUSIC

AV2

www.openlightbox.com

AV2

Step 1
Go to **www.openlightbox.com**

Step 2
Enter this unique code

AKPQVH05P

Step 3
Explore your interactive eBook!

Your interactive eBook comes with...

AV2 is optimized for use on any device

Read

- **Audio** Listen to the entire book read aloud
- **Videos** Watch informative video clips
- **Weblinks** Gain additional information for research
- **Try This!** Complete activities and hands-on experiments
- **Key Words** Study vocabulary, and complete a matching word activity
- **Quizzes** Test your knowledge
- **Slideshows** View images and captions
- **Share** Share titles within your Learning Management System (LMS) or Library Circulation System
- **Citation** Create bibliographical references following APA, CMOS, and MLA styles

This title is part of our AV2 digital subscription

1-Year K–5 Subscription
ISBN 978-1-7911-3320-7

Access hundreds of AV2 titles with our digital subscription.
Sign up for a FREE trial at www.openlightbox.com/trial

The digital components of this book are guaranteed to stay active for at least five years from the date of publication.

GOSPEL

Contents

I love music.

Gospel is my favorite kind of music.

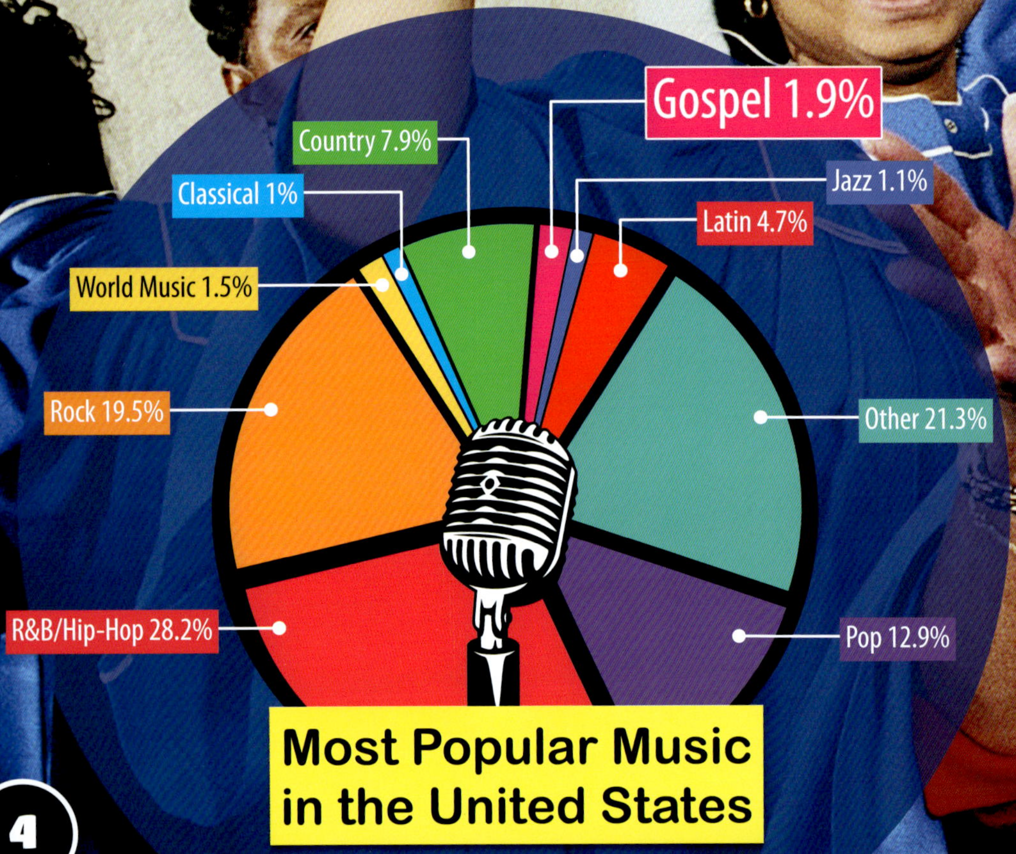

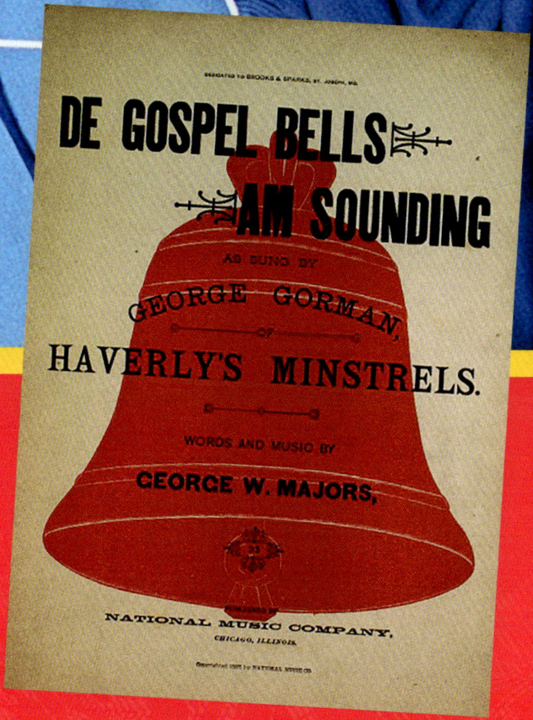

Gospel music began in the United States in the 1800s.

Gospel music came from songs sung by African American slaves.

They mixed their music with the songs they sang in church.

Many slaves sang these songs while they worked.

They made the songs sound happy to help them get through the day.

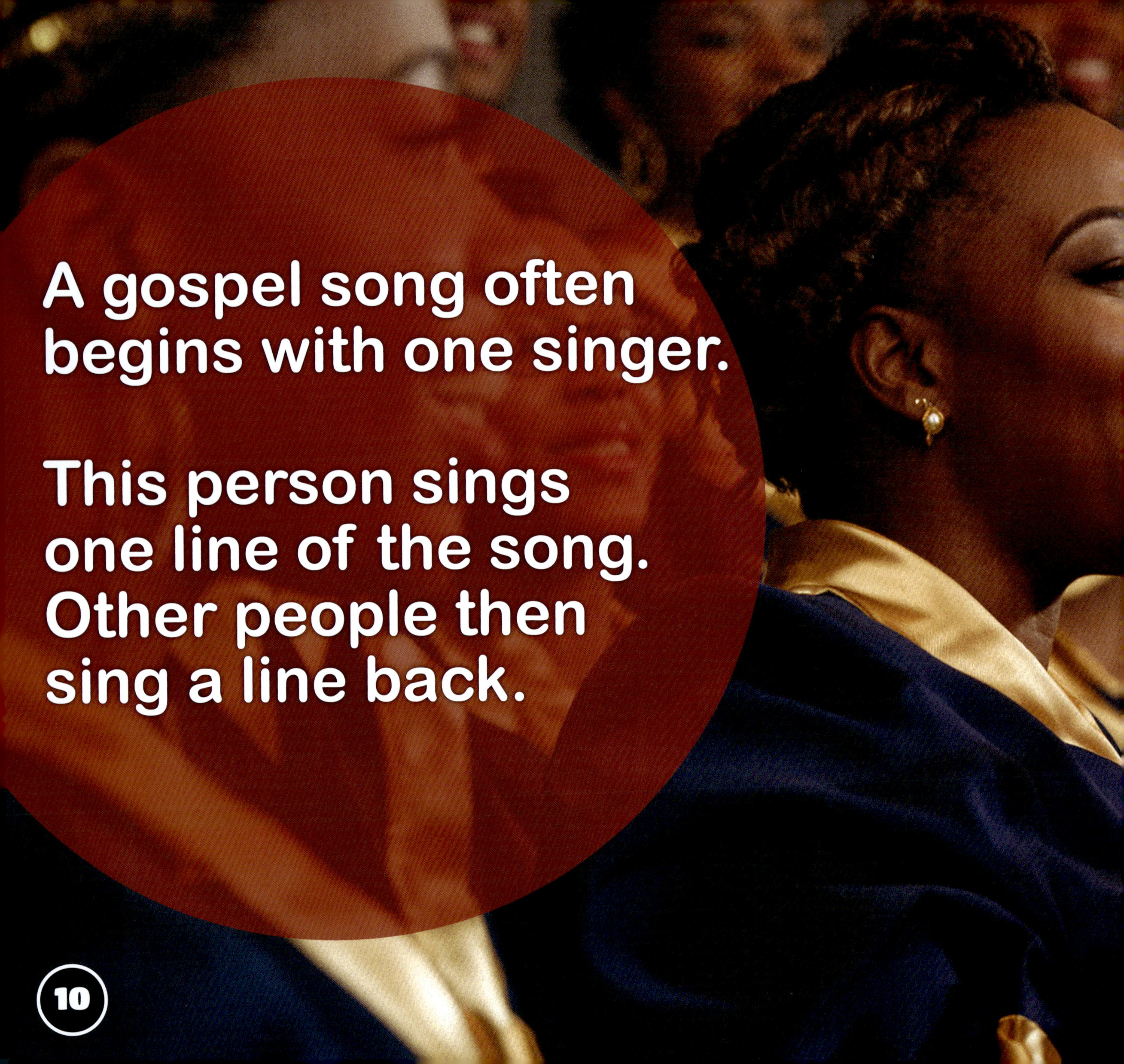

A gospel song often begins with one singer.

This person sings one line of the song. Other people then sing a line back.

The rest of the song continues in the same way.

Gospel songs have simple messages about faith and God.

They show hope for the future and joy in God’s love.

Voices are the most important instruments in gospel music.

Tambourines are sometimes played to help keep the beat.

I like to sing gospel music with my friends.

Together, we are a choir.

Singing in a choir teaches us how to work as a team.

Chicago is often called the home of gospel music.

The first gospel choir was formed here.

Today, gospel music is performed all over the world.

I love gospel music.

It stirs
my soul.

GOSPEL FACTS

These pages provide detailed information that expands on the interesting facts found in the book. They are intended to be used by adults as a learning support to help young readers round out their knowledge of each musical genre featured in the *My Favorite Music* series.

Pages 4–5

I love music. Gospel is my favorite kind of music. Music is the name given to sounds made with voices or musical instruments and put together in a way that conveys emotion. People use music to express themselves. Gospel music, in particular, is a way for people to express their religious feelings and beliefs. Over time, gospel music has been influenced by many types of popular music. However, it continues to be a way to express Christian faith as well.

Pages 6–7

Gospel music came from songs sung by African American slaves. Gospel music grew out of the diverse musical heritage of African Americans. When Africans were brought to the Americas as slaves, they brought rich musical traditions with them. Once in America, they were exposed to other types of music as well, especially those with religious themes. Over time, they applied the strong rhythms and structures of their traditional music to the music they heard in the Americas.

Pages 8–9

Many slaves sang songs while they worked. Most American slave owners required their slaves to attend regular church services, where they learned to sing traditional European hymns. To make a day of hard labor go faster, the slaves began to merge their own music with the hymns. They created a type of song known as the spiritual, which they would sing while working in the fields. In spirituals, they expressed hope that their faith would lead them to better lives. These songs laid the groundwork for gospel music.

Pages 10–11

A gospel song often begins with one singer. Gospel songs are often performed in a call-and-response format, a throwback to traditional African music. In call-and-response, one person leads the song by singing the first line of each set of lyrics solo. After each line is complete, the other singers sing a response to the leader. Gospel music is also known for its strong rhythms. Singers are often encouraged to clap and sway to the beat as they sing.

Pages 12–13

Gospel songs have simple messages about faith and God. Gospel songs reflect the history of African Americans, including their musical background from Africa, their challenging experiences in slavery, and their faith. Gospel lyrics are often simple, clear messages about hope, God's love, and Jesus Christ. Many gospel songs focus on a personal relationship with God.

Pages 14–15

Voices are the most important instruments in gospel music. Gospel music can be sung by soloists, duos, quartets, and choirs. Its singers often improvise and bring their own unique approach to each song. A variety of instruments can be incorporated into a performance. As traditional church instruments, organs and pianos are often used as accompaniment. Tambourines and drums help singers stay in time with the beat.

Pages 16–17

I like to sing gospel music with my friends. Creating music with others helps teach children cooperation, teamwork, and how to achieve goals. Children who regularly play music tend to have more confidence and get along better with others. Some students learn better in groups because they do not feel the pressure of having to learn on their own.

Pages 18–19

Chicago is often called the home of gospel music. Chicago is where gospel music began to gain a larger following. Much of this can be credited to Thomas A. Dorsey. Dorsey had a background as a blues and jazz musician and composer. After tragic events in his life, he began to write gospel music. He then set about founding the country's first gospel choir, at Ebenezer Baptist Church. With other noted musicians, such as acclaimed singer Mahalia Jackson, Dorsey began to promote gospel music throughout Chicago. Since these early days, interest in gospel music has spread around the world.

Pages 20–21

I love gospel music. Recent studies suggest that learning and practicing music can be beneficial to a child's ability to learn. Among these benefits are improved motor skills and dexterity, increased test scores, and even raised Intelligence Quotient, or IQ, scores. Learning music at an early age has also been shown to aid in language development and to improve reading and listening skills.

SIGHT WORDS

Research has shown that as much as 65 percent of all written material published in English is made up of 300 words. These 300 words cannot be taught using pictures or learned by sounding them out. They must be recognized by sight. This book contains 66 common sight words to help young readers improve their reading fluency and comprehension. This book also teaches young readers several important content words. These words are paired with pictures to aid in learning and improve understanding.

Page	Sight Words First Appearance
4	country, I, in, is, kind, most, my, of, other, states, the, world
5	began
6	American, by, came, from, songs
7	their, they, with
8	many, these, while
9	day, get, help, made, sound, them, through, to
10	a, back, begins, line, often, one, people, then, this
11	same, way
12	about, and, have
13	for, show
14	are, important
15	keep, sometimes
16	like, together, we
17	as, how, us, work
18	home
19	all, first, here, over, was
21	it

Page	Content Words First Appearance
4	classical, gospel, hip-hop, jazz, Latin, music, pop, R&B, rock, United States
6	slaves
7	church
10	person, singer
11	rest
12	faith, God, messages
13	future, hope, joy, love
14	instruments, voices
15	beat, tambourines
16	choir, friends
17	team
18	Chicago
21	soul

Published by Lightbox Learning Inc.
276 5th Avenue, Suite 704 #917
New York, NY 10001
Website: www.openlightbox.com

Library of Congress Cataloging-in-Publication Data
Names: Wilson, Sierra, author.
Title: Gospel / Sierra Wilson.
Description: New York : Lightbox Learning Inc., 2026. | Series: My favorite music | Audience: Grades 2-3
Identifiers: LCCN 2024048591 (print) | LCCN 2024048592 (ebook) | ISBN 9798874503079 (library binding) | ISBN 9798874503086 (paperback) | ISBN 9798874503093 (ebook other) | ISBN 9798874503116 (ebook other)
Subjects: LCSH: Gospel music--History and criticism--Juvenile literature.
Classification: LCC ML3187 .W55 2024 (print) | LCC ML3187 (ebook) | DDC 782.25/4--dc23/eng/20241015
LC record available at https://lccn.loc.gov/2024048591
LC ebook record available at https://lccn.loc.gov/2024048592

Printed in Guangzhou, China
1 2 3 4 5 6 7 8 9 0 29 28 27 26 25

042025
100924

Art Director: Terry Paulhus **Project Coordinator:** Heather Kissock